THE ESSENTIAL GUIDE TO PREPPING :

45 Survival Tips For Beginners

David Pearson

Pearson Press

This book is dedicated to all of those who seek a safer, happier, more fulfilled life – one that is free from fear and dependency.

CONTENTS

DAVID PEARSON

INTRODUCTION

HAVE YOU EVER SUFFERED A POWER FAILURE? Maybe a storm knocked down a few branches, took out some power lines, and you were without electricity for a few hours...

How many times did you enter a room during this power failure, flip the light switch, and then remember; "oh, right...the power's out." This isn't unusual. As a society, we have been dependent on all these little luxuries and conveniences our entire lives, to the point where we take many modern conveniences for granted.

Is it dark? Flip a switch. Thirsty? Grab a bottle of water from the fridge or turn on a tap. Life's most basic necessities - things that required lots of time and effort in order for our ancestors to survive - now take little more than a thought.

That is perhaps the most challenging component of planning for you and your family's survival in the event of an emergency. And it is also where this book deviates a bit from the more commonly written survival manuals.

I have come across literally thousands of survival manuals in my life. Some talk about food security, others stress the importance of building a shelter or installing generators. Interestingly, out of all those books, I've never come across one that talked about the importance of shoes and socks. Why? Because it's one of those simple things that people simply take for granted nowadays. But stop and think for a moment: If there were no stores, no malls, no place where you could buy footwear... what would you do if your shoes wore out? Assume that you've been wandering around for a week because a major flood has made you homeless, shelters have no room, and your shoes are wearing out. What would you do? See, it's the simple little oversights such as this that could endanger your life. I'm not kidding. You're walking around areas that are wet and muddy; areas that are crawling with parasites and disease, the holes in your shoes have abraded your skin, allowing a perfect avenue for infection.

There aren't any doctors or antibiotics. Suddenly, a minor little problem, something you may never really have given much thought to (other than how good your shoes look with your outfit), has put your life at risk. And if you have a family that depends upon you, you've put their life at risk as well.

These are the types of topics we will focus on in this guide. Of course, the basics like food, water and shelter will be covered, but even then, the primary consideration will be a common sense approach. It is likely that many of the things you will read here will cause you to slap your forehead and say, "Duh! Why didn't I think of that?"

The singular most important thing to keep in mind when assembling your survival plans is this: Preparation. I began talking about the conveniences that we have all been conditioned to take for granted. And when it comes to a natural disaster or civil disruption, your best and really, only chance is to have all your preparations ready in advance and in anticipation of an emergency situation. Think about it: Food? Everyone in your community needs that too. What would you be willing to do to feed your family if they were starving? Have you considered that there are going to be thousands of others just as desperate as you?

Perhaps, if you're lucky, you have the means to build a comprehensive shelter, to install tanks that hold thousands of gallons of diesel for your generators. In which case, this book...

...Is still for you. The focus of this book is on people of not-unlimited means to survive a natural disaster or similar calamity. In other words: everybody. Because no matter what precautions you take, what supplies you have stocked, they will eventually run out. And you'll be in the same boat as everyone else. Please don't misunderstand - if you have the ability to construct a purpose-built shelter, to stock hundreds of pounds of freeze-dried food, do so. Having such at your disposal in an emergency will greatly increase your chances of survival. Just remember: supplies run out, and the best shelter in the world is useless if you have to evacuate it.

What it boils down to, is if you don't have enough food before an emergency happens, your chances of getting it afterwards are almost nil.

You will note that at times throughout this book, I will refer to a particular item or process without going into great detail. There are simply too many different survival techniques to be encompassed in just one book. Just writing concise directions for preparing game animals for food and clothing would easily be an entire book by itself.

Stressing preparation and the little considered details are the focus of this book. In an emergency situation, neglect of just one minor detail can literally be the difference between life and death.

In all frankness, there is no book or manual that can prepare you for every possible contingency. There are too many imponderables. But what we will do in the following pages is help you markedly increase you and your family's chances of survival in even the most long-term, extreme of disasters.

THE ESSENTIALS: FOOD, WATER & SHELTER

BELIEVE IT OR NOT, you can survive without your cell phone. And in the event of a major civic disruption, you'll have to. But no matter who you are and where you live, without constant continuous access to food, water and shelter, you will not survive for long. Not just access; adequate access. Having enough food to keep from starving is fine for a while, but without adequate nutrition for an extended period of time, your body will weaken from the lack of essential vitamins and minerals.

To begin with, being in such a physically weakened state carries with it its own problems. Inability to perform the everyday tasks you'll need to perform; such as getting more food and water becomes far more difficult.

The need to fight off communicable diseases is a must. Your immune system uses energy just like your muscles do. If you find yourself in a survival situation, not only will your body be under an enormous amount of stress, but, you'll likely be exposed to many more pathogens, taxing your energy reserves even further.

You may recall from school some of the long-term implications of malnutrition: Scurvy, caused by a lack of Vitamin C. What type of climate do you live in? Many of us get our Vitamin C from citric sources; oranges and other fruit juices. If you live in a colder climate, you are not going to have access to citric fruits, so your options for getting Vitamin C have been cut in half. Now what?

Well, you're going to be fine because you have read this guide, and are properly prepared for almost any eventuality. Let's begin.

"Survival requires us to leave our prejudices at home.
It's about doing whatever it takes - and ultimately those with the
biggest heart will win."

— Bear Grylls

SHELTER

CHAPTER ONE

SHELTER

OUT OF THE THREE BASICS, shelter could perhaps be considered the easiest. Not as in easy to find or maintain, but insomuch as the lack of shelter (depending on your local climate) as it might be the least life-threatening.

In the following sections of this book, we will discuss the precautions you can take in order from the least severe to the most severe. That is to say, we will begin with the things you can do to prepare you for a minor disruption, and work our way up to the steps you can take during a major, long-term disaster.

1

HOME

As the saying goes, Home Sweet Home. It is the best, most basic part of your survival plan. Before we get into the meat, please keep this in mind: Whenever possible in a disaster situation, try to stay in your house (or apartment). In addition to being in the place where you will be most secure and most likely to have all your emergency supplies stored, your home is also a psychological touchstone. It is a place where you feel safe and secure. In a survival situation, never forget the importance of your mental well-being.

2

CLIMATE CONSIDERATIONS

There are some things to consider before you prepare your home as your primary survival shelter. First: what kind of climate do you live in? The challenges of someone living in North Dakota are markedly different than those of one living in Southern Florida. We'll focus on those living in colder climates and annotate as necessary.

In a structure like a house, you are protected against rain, wind, etc. Really, the only climatic aspect you have to be concerned with is cold. Assume you are without power. So the chances are very good that your only source of heat is your own body.

If possible, prepare to stay in your basement for a while. Select the smallest room that you and your family can comfortably fit in, or use tarps and blankets to cordon off a small section if your basement is one continuous room. If you live in an apartment, again, find not only the smallest room you can live in, but try to find one that does not have an exterior wall that faces outside.

What we are trying to do is get into a place that has the greatest amount of insulation between you and the cold. This is much easier in a basement, as once you go down three or four feet (again, depending somewhat on the region in which you live) the temperature stays relatively constant around 50 degrees Fahrenheit (About 10 degrees centigrade). Trying to keep warm where the ambient atmosphere is commonly bearable is much easier than in a loft on the 20th floor.

In you are in an apartment you can place blankets or similar on the floors, walls and even the ceiling if practical (as difficult as it may be, the ceiling is probably one of the best places you can insulate). Remember your high school physics? Heat rises.

Try to reduce drafts as much as possible, but do not try to make your living space airtight. You still need to breathe. You may recall a few years ago the United States government telling people that, in the event of a chemical or biological attack, to seal up their windows and doors with duct tape. Had such an attack occurred, those people might have survived the attack only to die of suffocation!

If you can, seal up most of the room, focusing on the area where you sleep. At a point farthest from there, make sure you can feel a little draft. That way, you know fresh oxygen is getting in, but also has a chance to mix with the existing air and warm up before you feel it.

If you are preparing a space that has a window, try not to cover it up permanently. First, remember what I said about stress and looking after your mental state? A little sunlight is a free source of Vitamin D and can do wonders for a depressed mood (and natural disasters can be pretty depressing). Finally, it's a lot easier to break a window than a wall. There are all kinds of circumstances in which you might have to evacuate your home. And chances are you're going to have to leave in a hurry. Going out a nearby window might be your only escape in a fire, or if you have an intruder. So leave yourself that escape whenever possible.

3

STAYING WARM

Blankets, coats, thermals, sweaters. Preparation. Have these items in abundance before an emergency takes place.

Fortunately this type of preparation (while important) is easy and cheap. You can get every one of these items from a thrift store for pennies on the dollar. Remember that often the best materials for staying warm are natural ones, wool and cotton allow your skin to breathe, and regulate your temperature much better than synthetic ones. In case of a fire, using natural materials is a much safer bet too. After washing, you can store these items in plastic garbage bags for when you need them.

4

HEAT SOURCES

You might live in an area that is so cold, that mere insulation isn't enough, and you require a source of heat. If you think this is you, please weigh options carefully as you will have to consider two very real threats: fire and toxic fumes. Remember, you're on your own. If your house catches fire, there won't be a fire department to come save you. With your house now gone, will you be able to acquire a new shelter?

If you've done a good job of sealing up drafts, how long before noxious gases build up from burning something? Everyone is aware that you can't burn gasoline, charcoal or wood indoors because of carbon monoxide fumes. Kerosene, natural gas and propane are safer, but you must keep in mind these gases also produce carbon monoxide when burned. If you need to make a heat source a part of your survival plan, make sure that you purchase a heater that has been specifically designed for indoor use. It is also important to ensure that when you purchase fuel for your heater that it is of the highest grade available, and is stored uncontaminated.

For example, with kerosene, anything less than K-1 (a term used to distinguish kerosene that is meant for use in things such as indoor heaters) could release soot and higher carbon monoxide thereby making your heater not just inefficient, but deadly. Are you storing your kerosene in a container that was designed for gasoline? If so, are you absolutely sure the container has never stored gasoline? Even the slightest amount of contamination will dramatically increase the amount of carbon monoxide released and introduce a very real risk of explosion too.

For those lacking the money or space for an indoor heater and an adequate supply of gas, an effective, somewhat inexpensive alternative is an alcohol stove. In addition to its usefulness in your shelter, it also has the benefit of being light and portable. There are numerous varieties of alcohol stoves available at most camping supply stores, and at your more comprehensively stocked retail outlets. These can also be easily sourced on the internet as well. We'll discuss this in greater detail in the "Bugging Out" section.

5

SECURITY

After your shelter is environmentally secure, the next thing you'll want to consider is physical security.

In the last few years, purpose-built shelters have become more popular and thus, more widely available. This is certainly an advantageous investment to make if you are capable of doing so. Remember, as with any contractor doing construction on your behalf, ensure that they have the proper qualifications and are willing to provide unbiased references.

However, many will not have the option of a designated shelter. This does not mean you can't make some modifications to your existing home to greatly enhance its physical security. If you have an apartment, your options in this area are probably quite limited. We will therefore focus the discussion on what you can do with your home.

Hopefully, you have a basement, and are basing your home shelter plans on that. If you lack a basement, the same basic rules will still apply.

Glass block windows: As far as deterring or repelling potential intruders, replacing your basement windows with glass block will greatly enhance the security of your shelter. Windows are an obvious, weak ingress point for an intruder. With glass block windows, breaking into your shelter not only becomes very difficult, but would be very noisy as well; giving you and your loved ones time to escape to a safer area.

In addition to the security aspect, glass block windows are excellent insulators. Having this type of window can help keep your shelter much warmer and reduce your energy needs. One more final advantage is that such a modification doesn't look out of place. Glass block windows are considered by many to be very stylish. Not only is your typical homeowner likely to be concerned with the esthetics, it's also important for reasons of concealment.

After all, the best physical security you can have in a civil crisis is not having anyone know you're there!

Polycarbonate (Lexan): Much like Plexiglas, Polycarbonate is a much stronger (and more expensive) alternative. An option for windows first floor and above, Polycarbonate is an immensely strong clear plastic used in things like the canopies on fighter jets. It's an option to be considered if you lack a basement, or can afford the enhanced security. If you can afford this option, keep in mind that Polycarbonate is vulnerable to UV rays (sunlight). Manufacturers sell Polycarbonate sheet specifically designed for outdoor use, with a UV coating. Even short-term exposure to sunlight will substantially weaken Polycarbonate.

High-strength security door: After the windows, the only other point of ingress to your shelter is through the door. Obviously your budget will dictate how much door strength you can purchase, but try to obtain at least a sturdy, metal door that has a peephole. Eventually, someone will have to leave the shelter, and if others remain, it would be nice to be able to verify the identity of whoever is trying to get back in.

6

LIGHTING & COMMUNICATIONS

No matter the size and sophistication of your shelter, you'll not get much done in it if you can't see. As with so many things, your budget will largely determine how well you can look after these needs, but at the very least you'll need some illumination and energy for that illumination.

Flashlights: There are many varieties of flashlights that have self-contained generators and feature a little crank to power them. They are not terribly expensive, and you should include at least three or four in your survival kit. Look for the type with LED lamps in them as this type of bulb not only consumes less energy (meaning you'll burn less of those valuable calories while cranking it) but LED bulbs last almost forever compared to conventional bulbs. They usually provide brighter light too.

The next option is conventional flashlights or lanterns using standard or rechargeable batteries. Not the best option as you'll soon need to recharge the batteries. This presents a whole host of new problems. As with standard batteries you buy, this might be acceptable in a short-term emergency, but since you don't know what disaster will become long term, it's better to invest your money in lighting that is self-powered.

Candles: Potentially dangerous, candles only provide light for a short time. There are candles available that have been expressly designed for emergencies and will burn for an extended period of time, but the risk of fire remains. Whereas there really isn't much risk of toxic fumes, if your shelter has little ventilation, then your candles are burning what is likely a very low oxygen supply to begin with. I don't recommend them, but if you do decide to make candles a part of your survival plan, be sure to take the proper precautions.

Fire Extinguishers: Even without the candles mentioned above, there are still many other risks from fire. And the most important thing to remember is that if there is a fire, you're on your own; it's not likely there will be a fire department available to help you. Therefore, you would have to deal with a fire by yourself and as quickly as possible. That means a fire extinguisher. Keep in mind, if you use an ABC fire extinguisher, (the kind designed for ALL fires and the kind you SHOULD use) in an enclosed space, the white solution that comes out to extinguish the fire is carbon dioxide - the same gas that comes out of your mouth when you exhale. Release of such an amount of carbon dioxide can displace the oxygen in your shelter (just like the fire itself!), so be sure to open up some ventilation after you use it, only after you have made sure the fire is completely out. A fresh blast of air could re-start your fire.

Emergency Radio: Just like the flashlight, try to obtain one that has a self-contained generator with a crank. Any natural disaster can snowball and lead to even greater challenges. It could be anything; an earthquake that starts a fire or a thunderstorm that knocks out your town's warning alarms so you wouldn't know about an ensuing flood. Even with cell phones and internet, radio is still the best way to inform a populace about an emergency. Emergency food distribution and evacuation orders are important bits of information that your life may depend upon, information you'll be ignorant of without outside communications. In an emergency, leave your radio on continuously for at least the first 48 hours, and further as events warrant.

7

CLEANERS & DISINFECTANTS

Human beings are not the cleanest of creatures - a problem that can be magnified by being forced to live in close quarters without the benefit of regular access to water for bathing. Bacteria forms easily. Viruses have a much less inhospitable environment. Combined with added stress, your body is much more susceptible to disease during an emergency. Unlikely access to medical care only exacerbates this problem.

Regular cleaning and disinfecting of your living area and all its accoutrements is vital to your long-term survival. It would be very unfortunate to survive a natural disaster only to succumb to a viral infection days later. You do not need to use commercial cleaners or bleach in order to disinfect, and actually, bleach is not recommended for use as a cleaning product due to the fumes it releases, which are considered a health hazard. Hydrogen Peroxide, vinegar and baking soda are excellent multipurpose cleaners, and are considered safe enough to use even for other purposes outside of cleaning. Hydrogen peroxide has been found to be effective in killing bacteria, including E. coli. Please note if you choose to use hydrogen peroxide (along with baking soda and vinegar), do keep it in its own bottle. The bottle used must also be opaque (dark) in order to for it to be kept active. If you plan to use the hydrogen peroxide on wounds, it is important to note that it should not be used on cuts as a first line of defense as it oxidizes the cells and makes healing more difficult. Vinegar while pungent, also makes an excellent cleaner, and its strong scent dissipates once it dries. It can be used in combination with hydrogen peroxide as a produce wash due to its anti-microbial properties, and effectively kills most bacteria including E. coli, Salmonella, Shigella, and Listeria. Just be sure to use these cleaners individually, rather than in the same bottle. Much more about this can easily be found online if you feel so inclined. Not only will regular cleaning significantly reduce your chance of infection, it will give you something to do. As usual, never underestimate that aspect of morale in a crisis.

8

IMPORTANT PAPERS

In the middle of a crisis, your social security card may seem of little importance, but it's not. Try to keep in mind, AFTER the disaster... You'll still need these documents. Especially things like your homeowner's insurance policy. Most people keep these important documents in a secure place like a fireproof box already. Well, keep doing that. You might want to add a bit of cash and other items as well, such as gold or silver coins.

Prepping your home to serve as a shelter is the first and easiest step in preparing for an emergency. Even if you are limited by budget, the above mentioned are but a few of the simple things you can do that will greatly increase your chances of survival. As with all the advice in this book, think. Think about your particular situation and imagine what things you'll need when you can no longer get the things you need easily.

9

CAR

A far less desirable alternative to your home is a car. Your car can be primarily considered a fallback in the event your shelter becomes uninhabitable or you need to evacuate. Easier to seal against the elements, a car has the advantage of being a smaller space. Except for the most extreme temperatures, a properly bundled family in a car can produce enough body heat to not require an additional heat source.

Even then, as long as you have fuel, your car can provide you with heat. It's also a source of electricity; at the very least for charging cell phones and the like. In a situation where you have to evacuate, a car obviously has its uses. But don't become too dependent on your car as a means of escape. In a major crisis, what's usually the first thing to happen? The roads clog and traffic backs up. Prepare to travel on foot, which is what you'll likely be doing after you run out of gas, anyway.

If using your car for a shelter and occasional heat, don't forget about carbon monoxide poisoning. DO NOT run your car in an enclosed space. Furthermore, don't run your car in place (let it idle) for more than 10 or 15 minutes at a time. Your engine could overheat and sustain damage. Keep in mind also, if food is difficult to get, can you imagine how hard car repairs will be?

You'll also want to consider how visible you might be in a car. Just about anyone can walk up and see who you are, what supplies you might be carrying, etc. An automobile isn't very secure from attack, either. In summary, a car can be a shelter backup and a short-term energy supply. However it does leave you vulnerable to refugees and severe weather events, like tornadoes. Base your survival plans with these drawbacks in mind.

10

TENTS [AND OTHER TEMPORARY SHELTERS]

Later, in the "Bugging Out" section, I will address tents in greater detail, but for now they are obvious additions to any survival plan, and thus bear mention here.

A tent or tarp can be used if, for some reason, your primary shelter should become unlivable - even if only temporarily. If you have a well-stocked shelter, and moving all those supplies would be impractical, having the materials to erect a nearby shelter can be quite handy.

As usual, if you can afford a space-age tent with neoprene seals and the like - good. You'll want to get, of course, the highest quality tent you can afford, but some of the most important considerations are weight and size. Remember: Preparation. Circumstances may occur that force you away from your primary shelter. Preparing for such an eventuality by having a small, lightweight tent goes towards achieving that goal. As I said, we'll cover this topic in greater detail later in the book.

If your budget restricts you from purchasing a tent, a good alternative is merely a large, plastic tarp and some nylon rope. As for the tarp, plastic is the best bet due to its waterproof properties and it's also lightweight. Canvas is not only heavy, it's also more prone to leakage and mould. Nylon rope is similarly lightweight, strong and waterproof. This is important, traditional fiber rope will rot and weaken after repeatedly getting wet.

These are the three main components when considering the shelter portion of your survival plan. You should think of them in order of importance. And given that circumstances could force you to abandon any one of them at any time, you should have contingency plans as well. Are there places in your general area where you and your family could take shelter if you had to? Friends and relatives are probably options you would utilize before resorting to your car or a tent; No, I meant more along the lines of some final fallback options such as an abandoned building, or if you live near a park, a cave or something similar.

It might sound ridiculous to think of such things, but remember: Preparation. Disasters and emergencies are by definition, unexpected events. You know the saying - Expect the unexpected. Expect that you will be forced from your first three shelter options and at least think about what you might do if that were to happen. It doesn't have to be perfect, and resorting to such an option certainly carries immense risks, but in a crisis, with rain and temperatures falling - having at least an outline of a plan could save your life. Even if it's just someplace with a roof, to get out of the rain and give you time to rest and think could make all the difference.

"There's no such thing as survival of the fittest. Survival of the most adequate, maybe. It doesn't matter whether a solution's optimal. All that matters is whether it beats the alternative."

— Peter Watts

?

FOOD

CHAPTER TWO
FOOD

GOING IN ASCENDING ORDER OF IMPORTANCE, we come next to food. We're out of the rain, we're warm and we're secure from bandits - now, in order to continue surviving, we'll need nutrients.

This is yet another area where you are limited only by how much you're willing and capable of spending. And again, you really don't have to spend a whole lot in order to secure a good measure of food security. We'll begin with simple, short-term food solutions and move up to the long-term steps you should take.

Frozen food is a great solution for emergencies lasting less than 48 hours or if you have a well-fueled generator or solar panels - in other words, not a very good solution at all. I mention this because I have read survival guides that actually recommend stocking up on frozen food for an emergency. In most disasters, power is usually one of the first things to go. Unless you live in a climate that is cold year-round, frozen food is not advisable.

11

CANNED GOODS

In the short and medium term, you won't find a more effective or inexpensive method of meeting your dietary needs than food in a can. You can get all the proteins, carbohydrates, fats, vitamins and minerals you'll need in foods that taste good to you (a delicious meal during a crisis can be a wonderful stress reliever). In most cases, canned food is already cooked (make sure you get canned food that is already cooked) and while it may not be as palatable when unheated, it can be eaten as is and is just as nutritious. It is even healthier, cheaper and tastier should you can it yourself.

Be sure when purchasing canned food for your survival kit that you check the expiration dates and get food that will remain fresh for the longest possible time. Visit different stores, or the same store on different days to find the freshest prepared canned foods. Once you have prepared your food kit, don't forget to rotate the food regularly. Take out the older cans and replace them with fresh ones. Be a good sport, and donate the older, but still unexpired cans to your local food bank.

The topic of proper nutrition is one that is too comprehensive to go into detail here, just keep in mind when purchasing your emergency food to get enough of all the proper nutrients. Remember earlier when I talked about Scurvy? Get plenty of cans of fruit enriched with Vitamin C. Get plenty of foods high in fiber. If you have gastrointestinal difficulties, and you didn't pack any Pepto-Bismol, you could end up with problems.

In today's modern society, there are numerous diets out there that counsel you to avoid this food or that, and that's fine. Because in modern society if you have a problem, there's plenty of other foods available; there are doctors and hospitals if your problem is really serious. But the rules are different in a disaster.

Although many people have been led to believe that things like carbs or fat are things to be avoided, your body actually needs these substances in order to survive. When selecting foods for your survival kit, avoid canned goods that are advertised as low-fat or low-carb. As I said, you need these nutrients to survive, but more than that, in a crisis, you'll be under a lot of stress. You'll quite likely be more physically active. Your body is probably going to need all the calories you can get. If you're somewhere cold, this becomes even more important. Even if you aren't really moving, in the cold, your body still burns a lot of calories just to stay warm. Explorers and scientists who work outdoors in the Antarctic usually consume around 5000 calories a day. Trust me, in an emergency situation, your waistline will be the least of your worries. Stock up on food that is as healthy, tasty and nutritionally dense as possible.

Also be sure to try and find canned goods that are marked BPA free, especially important should the crisis become a longer-term one. If you are able to can your food yourself, you should be able to limit this entirely as glass doesn't contain BPA. Another drawback to keep in mind about canned food is that it's not very portable in large quantities. Not only the weight of the metal cans, but the fully prepared food inside those cans weighs quite a bit on their own. Canned goods are a great option for your shelter, but not so much if you have to travel. Depending on what other supplies you may have to carry, you will likely only carry enough food for a few days or so. Carrying that extra weight will cost you more calories in the long run as well.

In the end, canned goods are an excellent choice for your survival plans. Kept cool, they will be usable for a long time. Proper storage can also help them stay good past the expiration date. I don't recommend consuming expired food, but it is a commonly accepted fact that most canned foods, while perhaps not as tasty, remain edible long after the date on the can.

Oh, and one more thing: Make sure you purchase several mechanical can openers as well. Several, because as you might be aware, mechanical can openers sometimes rust. It would be very inconvenient if, one year into a long-term disaster your one and only can opener broke and you were stuck having to bash open your canned peaches on a rock, spilling most of them in the process and attracting vermin.

12

DRIED GRAINS, BEANS & SEEDS

For basic nutritional needs, dried goods are a recommended choice from the short to long term. Rice, oatmeal, dried beans and wheat all have adequate amounts of carbohydrates and protein, along with some vitamins as well. However, certain dried foods can be difficult to prepare.

Foods like rice or dried beans need water and heat to make them edible. For staples like wheat or dried corn, you'll need a mill to grind the grains into flour, which also needs other ingredients and heat for cooking. In spite of these disadvantages, you should seriously consider grains as a part of your long-term survival kit. Purchased in bulk, they are quite inexpensive. Stored in airtight containers, and kept cool and dry, it is possible for grains to remain edible for twenty years or more.

A valuable product to have if you decide to use this option is oxygen absorbers. These are little packets of an oxygen absorbing substance that you place inside the container with your food. It absorbs the oxygen, which is what promotes spoilage. They are also cheap and easy to find on the internet. The internet is also an excellent place to shop for grain mills. Try to find one that is manually operated and is made out of stainless steel. Even if you don't plan on storing dried grains in your survival kit, if you can afford it, purchase a grain mill. You never know what the future might hold, and getting a hold of corn or wheat seeds is likely to be far easier than obtaining a grain mill during a civil disruption. Better to have it and not need it, than to need it and not have it.

Some grains also have the advantage of being sproutable, meaning that if they are left to soak overnight and then rinsed with a little water every 8 hours or so for a few days, they will begin to sprout. This gives them alternate uses and also makes them more nutritious. Sprouting is done indoors, and requires little space, even a small window ledge will do. Using them in this way also means that you don't necessarily need a grain mill (unless you wish to dehydrate them and then mill them down for baking). Once sprouted, these grains can be eaten as is, or ground down and baked in various recipes. Chickpeas, mung beans, black beans, adzuki beans, buckwheat groats, kidney beans, dried green peas and red lentils are all sproutable. As well - alfalfa seed, sunflower seed, red clover seed, watercress seed, barley seed and hard red winter wheat seed are also sproutable and make an excellent alternative to lettuce. All that is needed is a jar (or sprouting/nut milk bag), a little clean water, a few days time and a little sunlight towards the end of their growth to green them up. The only exception to this is if you choose to grow the hard winter wheat or barley to a grass form (which is very nutritious), then some soil and a small tray in which to grow will be required. Just make sure that if you decide to use these as a part of your food storage, that you test out your seeds/beans/grains beforehand to make sure that they are still active. If this concerns you, you may want to consider ordering them online from a place sells them for the sole purpose of sprouting, rather than their traditional cooking uses. Keep in mind these beans/seeds need to be dry (they have not been canned), and ideally need to be ones made for human consumption (rather than grains designated for horse or cattle feed).

13

OATMEAL

I've mentioned this one separately due to a university study I read less than a year ago. Regardless of what the expiration date says on the container, oatmeal can stay edible for more than ten years if stored properly (like everything else, in a cool dry place). Oatmeal has the benefit of being edible by just soaking it in water for a period of time. Sure, it's much better if you cook it, but you can get by in a pinch without.

Healthy and filling, oatmeal is pretty cheap. You can get enough to last you for a month for less than ten dollars. And finally, oatmeal is very lightweight when it's dry. If need be, you can carry a significant amount should you be forced to travel. Just remember to be prepared for this by having several airtight, lightweight containers in which to carry your supply.

14

DEHYDRATED
& FREEZE-DRIED FOODS

Dehydrated and Freeze-dried foods are your best choices for the most long-term disasters. With shelf lives of ten, twenty years or more, dehydrated and freeze dried foods have the additional benefits of being light weight and low volume. A case of large (#10) cans of normal food might have as many as 40 or 50 servings and weigh as much as 25 pounds. Whereas a case of freeze-dried food of the same type might contain 150 servings or more and probably weigh less than five pounds.

The principal differences are in preparation, shelf life and cost. Dehydrated foods tend to be a single type of food, such as rice or chicken. No additional ingredients, no seasonings. Freeze dried foods are usually more complete meals, such as Beef stew or Spaghetti and Meatballs. Dehydrated is cheaper than freeze-dried, and usually even cheaper than common canned food that you find in the grocery store.

Freeze-dried has the longest shelf life, is considered to be the tastiest after extremely long-term storage and is the lightest and most compact (significantly more so than dehydrated food). Available at camping supply stores and on many survival-oriented websites, these types of goods are important additions to any survival kit.

These advantages must be weighed against one major drawback, however: They require water to reconstitute them and heat for cooking. As their name implies, Dehydrated and Freeze-dried foods have had up to 98% of their water content removed. They must be cooked in water, or reconstituted, to make them edible - with the exception of dehydrated fruits, seaweeds, or sprouted grains. Good long-term food options, sure, but you'll need to stock more resources; water, a heat source and energy for that heat. As with oatmeal, light to carry in large quantities, you'll still need to carry or be able to find water if you need to travel. Dehydrated fruits, seaweeds and sprouted grains can be kept long term, as long as they are appropriately stored in a dry cool area, and can be eaten without rehydration, or cooking.

Another benefit to dehydrated foods as opposed to freeze-dried foods is that they can be easily prepared at home, ahead of time, before a crisis situation. Dehydrators can be purchased rather inexpensively new or second hand. If you are even a little bit handy you can build a solar one, which does not require additional electricity, and can be used in a crisis situation if needed. Free plans for a variety of models can be found online.

15

MRE'S (MEALS READY TO EAT)

Finally, lets discuss things like MRE's (which are used by the army) and energy bars. MRE's have the advantage of a very long shelf life if stored properly, and are very convenient. You don't need extra water or a heat source to cook them. Some MRE's come with a chemical pack, that when activated, generates heat and allows you to enjoy a hot, nutritious meal without any other additional resources.

However, there are numerous drawbacks. MRE's are quite expensive. Even purchased in bulk, a single MRE can run as high as ten dollars retail. They're bulky and not particularly light. Combined with other supplies that you would likely carry if you have to travel, you would have difficulty carrying any more than a few days' supply of MRE's. While they aren't necessarily a bad choice for your survival kit, they are not a particularly good one either, especially as a long-term solution.

Energy bars are a good option, especially if you need to travel. They're small and compact and most are nutritionally dense. However, while you might supplement your survival kit with energy bars, you certainly shouldn't make them a basic component of your survival kit. Very few varieties provide anywhere near complete nutrition, and worse, they're usually loaded with sugar.

This is something (not only for energy bars) that you should avoid. Obviously, in a survival situation, sugar can be a source of quick energy, but not a very good one. The energy boost doesn't last as long as the energy you'd get from a can of peaches, for example. But nutritional deficiency isn't our major concern here. Think about preparation - If you're eating foods laced with sugar, what about your teeth? In a long term crisis there would be no dentists, and if you get a cavity, it will go untreated and likely develop into an abscess. From there you could easily develop sepsis (a nasty infection), which could become fatal. True preparation requires an enormous amount of foresight.

It probably wouldn't occur to someone that eating an energy bar could end up being a threat to their lives, but these are the harsh realities during a longer-term crisis.

16

VITAMIN & MINERAL SUPPLEMENTS

Buy them! Make sure you always have plenty ready and make sure they're as fresh as can be (just like with canned goods, "rotate your stock"). Multivitamin pills are an absolutely essential part of any survival plan, whether it's for your shelter survival kit, or your traveling survival kit.

Even under normal circumstances, a lot of people today don't get the proper amounts of vitamins and minerals - and that's under the best of circumstances. During a crisis, this will likely get worse. Did you know you could eat three regular meals a day; meals that meet all your caloric requirements, and still starve to death? We don't think much of this now because of modern refrigeration and transportation methods - we can easily have a large variety of different foods in our diet (but I assure you, 100 years ago, people weren't getting much Kiwi fruit in New York). Today, with these modern conveniences, it's fairly easy to get most of the essential nutrients we need.

In a crisis, this won't be the case. If you don't have adequate food supplies stored in preparation, or those supplies run out, the only food available will be that which is local. That means you won't be eating oranges or bananas if you live in the North. No apples or potatoes if you're in the tropics. Therefore, make sure you replace the nutrients you're no longer getting from these foods with multivitamin supplements. As a side note, it should be said, it is always to your advantage to become familiar with your local farmers, neighbors and those you could trade with should the need arise – it's all about who you know.

The other huge advantage is portability (detailed later in the "Bugging Out" section). Sometimes survival could involve traveling, even on foot. This means you'll want to carry as little weight as possible. First of all, having Multivitamin supplements greatly opens up your options for carrying food. Rather than carrying many different foods to get all of your required nutrients, you could carry one or two bulk foods that are high in protein and carbohydrates and just the vitamins, too. For example, a large amount of oatmeal along with multivitamins, and you're set for a good long while.

Herbs and mushrooms are also another excellent alternative, and weigh much less than traditional vitamin supplements. They grow freely in almost every place in the world and can be foraged or grown in your garden. Herbs also have an excellent shelf life when stored dried in a cool place, or tinctured (preserved in alcohol, or glycerin). There is a wide array of uses for herbs - everything from aiding the flu, headaches, insomnia (another morale booster), rashes, wounds and respiratory conditions. They also contain many easily absorbable forms of vitamins and minerals. Some excellent choices for your pantry would be Nettles, Calendula, Echinacea, Peppermint, Reishi Mushroom, Skullcap and Dandelion root. There are many more that would be much too much to mention here. Having a field guide on hand for medicinal herbs and mushrooms local to your area would be an excellent asset. Most of them have quite a palatable taste, and make an excellent alternative to tea or coffee, or even soup (and are more nutritious too!).

I feel it would be a shame for me not to mention the benefit of dried seaweeds with their multitude of uses and exceptional nutritional value. Seaweed can be used to aid in wound healing (applied directly across an open wound, like a band-aid). Kelp (and the iodine it contains) has been used to help protect against radiation poisoning (in this case, more is not better, as too much kelp can affect your thyroid). As little as a ¼ tsp dried and sprinkled on your food is sufficient. Kelp can also be found in tablet form (although I would consult with your doctor for proper usage).

Last but not least – honey. Honey has been used for millennia, as a sweetener, as medicine and as an excellent source of vitamins. Manuka honey in particular is excellent for wound care and aiding in the recovery of illness.

17

HOMEGROWN

Unless you can invest upwards of $100,000 dollars on a huge supply of freeze-dried food (plus another few hundred grand to construct a shelter big enough to hold all that food), your food supply will eventually run out in a long-term disaster. Preparing for such a long-term disruption is definitely something you should take into account when planning your kit.

Fortunately, this is both inexpensive and easy. Packets of seeds are quite cheap. As with canned goods, seeds expire. If they do, they won't necessarily rot, they just won't grow. Do some research, find out what types of plants are suitable for growing in your area and in surrounding areas. Remember, you might not be able to stay with your primary shelter. Try to select plants that are quite hardy, require minimal water, and, if possible, will grow in partial or full shade. The reason for this is we want to conceal our garden as much as possible. (Growing indoors would be ideal, but not really feasible - such growing techniques require a great deal of energy).

Purchase some gardening tools, both full size as well as the small ones that people typically use to work on flower gardens. The regular tools are for your primary shelter, and the mini-tools are in case you should need to travel.

There are many, many techniques and options when it comes to growing your own food, far more than we have the space for here. Suffice it to say that supplies for growing your own food should be a basic, integral part of your survival kit.

18

GAME & DOMESTIC ANIMALS

Again, this is an enormously encompassing topic without room to go into detail, but its importance at least bears mention. Meat is an excellent source of protein, and you never know what circumstances could come about to leave you with no other option. If you face a situation where your food runs out or must be abandoned and you are unable to forage more, hunting might be the only thing that saves you from starvation.

This is another area in which preparation is key. You could not walk into a gun store today, purchase a rifle, walk out into the field and be an instantly successful hunter. Likewise, you cannot wait until a disaster occurs and then decide to learn how to hunt. You'll be taking large and unnecessary risks if you do.

Just like everything else we've covered so far, your budget will be the biggest determining factor, but here are some points to keep in mind when tailoring your survival plan to include the possibility of hunting:

19

CHOOSING A FIREARM

A light, small caliber rifle is your ideal choice, like a .22 (Guns are designated by the caliber, or diameter of the bullet in inches. Thus, a .22 has a bullet diameter of 220 thousandths of an inch). First, both .22 rifles and shells (bullets) are quite inexpensive, durable, reliable and easy to use. While such a rifle wouldn't be suitable for bringing down something as large as a deer, for example, your opportunities for acquiring something like a deer are remote to the point as to not justify the need for a larger rifle. Your most likely target will probably be smaller; rabbits, squirrels, birds, etc. I'm not recommending against investing in a more powerful firearm - you never know what you might need - it's just that in most instances you will find a smaller caliber weapon better suited to your needs.

Keep in mind as well, there are a lot of hunters in the world and your chances of successfully competing against them for scarce food resources are pretty low. If you're in the woods after a deer, and a skilled, armed hunter is after that same deer, you're chances of winning aren't very good to begin with. Furthermore, that hunter may be trying to save his family from starvation, just as you are doing. If you get between him and that food, what do you think he's likely to do?

Don't forget to purchase gun oil and cleaning supplies for your survival kit. Especially if you are traveling, your gun will be exposed to the elements. Regular cleaning and oiling will be vital to the longer-term usefulness of your firearm. If it breaks, you'll have a heck of a time replacing it.

20

A WORTHY ALTERNATIVE

Although a very difficult option, I'm going to mention it because it offers so many advantages: Bow hunting. Whether with a longbow or a crossbow, if you have the time and resources to learn this valuable skill, I highly encourage it for a couple of reasons. First, using bullets to hunt means another consumable, hard-to-replace supply you need to worry about. Arrows, if not damaged beyond repair, can be used again and again. Very difficult to run out of. And if you have the wherewithal, you at least have the possibility of constructing your own arrows in a pinch. Without specialized equipment and yet more supplies, you can't make your own bullets.

The second big advantage is sound. We've touched on this topic previously, but one thing you always need to keep in mind in a crisis is to not draw attention to yourself. If you have resources, and some nearby desperate person does not, trouble can result. The firing of a gun can be heard for many miles, essentially advertising your presence and position to anyone in the surrounding area. If it's practical, eliminating that noise by using a bow weapon is an important survival technique.

21

FARM ANIMALS

Another well-considered survival food plan is the keeping of farm animals. Now, while a herd of cows would be wonderful sources of both milk and meat, they are hardly practical. An immense amount of supplies and space is required to keep cows, not to mention it's pretty obvious to any casual passers-by. Obviously, keeping animals is something you would have to be prepared for long in advance of any emergency. And such an option is only good as long as you can remain at a more permanent shelter. But if you can utilize this recommended option, here are a few tips:

Chickens are a fine choice for this purpose. They don't consume much space, they don't have tremendously specific dietary needs and in addition to the meat they can provide, they lay eggs almost continuously, providing a constant, daily source of protein. If you have a garden, their droppings can be an excellent fertilizer. Garden waste - inedible leaves and such, can be used as chicken feed.

Goats are another desirable choice as an emergency food supply. They require more space, but their range of diet is even greater than a chicken's. And like a chicken, they provide constant nutrition in the form of milk and cheese as well as meat.

If planning on raising animals as part of your survival kit, be mindful when setting up the pen where they will reside. Not just the standard things like guarding against predators or proper drainage, but how visible it is from a distance. How are the acoustics? How far away can you hear your chickens clucking? Can you adjust the animal enclosure to reflect less sound? (Soft surfaces are good – if one wall is solid, stack some hay bales in front of it to attenuate the sound) Place your pen in a stand of trees, weave vegetation through the wires if you have a fence.

Walk a distance away from your animal enclosure, experiment, see what works as effective disguise and what doesn't. IF you feel you can trust them, invite family or friends to see how far away they can notice your pen.

Finally, smell. You won't be able to eliminate it entirely, but you should do your best to control it. Clean your animal pen regularly, and bury the waste or recycle it as fertilizer.

"When walking alone in a jungle of true darkness, there are three things that can show you the way: instinct to survive, the knowledge of navigation, creative imagination. Without them, you are lost."

— Toba Beta

WATER

CHAPTER THREE
WATER

SAVING THE MOST IMPORTANT FOR LAST: Water. Depending on your body fat, metabolism and overall health, you can survive for a week or more without food. Depending on environmental conditions, you can survive indefinitely without shelter. But no one can go more than a few days without water. The good thing about water is that it's virtually everywhere. The bad news is that only a small percentage is actually drinkable.

In spite of this downside, water is a fairly easy thing to prepare. The first thing to determine is how much water you need. The answer is the same for all of us: As much as you can get. Most experts recommend at least a gallon a day, per person for drinking, cooking and bathing. I have found that when most people read that, the first thing they think is "I don't need water for bathing; in an emergency I'll have bigger things to worry about than being dirty." True. However, there are things like disease and infection. Never discount the importance of good hygiene during a disaster.

The cleaner you, your clothes, your living area, your cooking and eating utensils are, the less opportunity for bacteria to incubate. The fewer avenues of infection the better. Getting a little nick on your finger, and then touching a pot handle that is crawling with bacteria can be as fatal as being consumed by a flood. The process might be slower and more painful, but the end result is the same.

22

OBTAINING & STORING WATER

Now, some guidance on obtaining and storing water:

Every time you visit the supermarket, pick up one of those gallons of bottled water. Usually they sell for less than a dollar, and it's easy to build up a large supply quickly and inexpensively. Make sure you get spring water and NOT distilled water. Distilled water has had all the minerals removed, minerals that are vital to your health. Drinking distilled water, over a short period of time, will leach the water soluble minerals from your body, causing significant health problems.

Regular sized bottled water is just as acceptable, but is not really worth the extra expense. If you can, purchase several milk crates and store 4 gallon jugs in each. This allows you to stack your water gallons, giving you the ability to store more in a smaller space. Some water has an expiration date printed. Ignore this. Kept sealed in a cool, dry place, water will never spoil as long as it remains uncontaminated. You should also become familiar with your local watershed, and springs. Spring water is the best water for drinking, and is how our ancestors survived before the invention of indoor plumbing. If you don't know where a spring is located, there is a website called findaspring.com that lists local springs, added by people around the world. Another more reliable way is to ask around your community, especially your elders. Ask where they used to get their water from, and if they know the location of a nearby spring. You will most surely get some valuable information from them, as they grew up much more in touch with their environment and are an excellent ally in helping you to plan for your family's safety.

There are a few products on the market that purify water for you, there is the lifesaver straw, the lifesaver bottle and the katadyn bottle, as well as a few others. If you have the means to invest in one of these, I believe it is definitely worth including in your survival pack, both for at home and in your bug out bag.

23

PREPARING YOUR OWN

A cost-saving alternative is to prepare your own water. You can reuse pop, juice or milk jugs, but you have to clean them extremely thoroughly with hot and soapy water. Cleaning and rinsing more than once is definitely recommended. You must also ensure that the lid is still in good condition and can provide a good seal. If filling you jugs from a tap that has treated or, "city" water, no further action is required. But, if you're getting your water from a well (and if you have a well, long-term water needs won't be as much of a concern as they might be to others) or something similar in which the water hasn't been treated, then you will need to treat it yourself to prevent the growth of bacteria. (Water-born illnesses are very common during disasters; treat your water supply with the utmost care).

Using plain chlorine bleach, (DO NOT use the kinds that are scented; the chemicals used for the scent can be harmful) measure 8 drops (about1/8 of a teaspoon) for every one gallon of water. Reseal the jug and shake it to thoroughly disperse the bleach. DO NOT drink it for at least half an hour. This is to allow time for the bleach to kill the bacteria present. After this time, the water should still have just the slightest bleach odor. Make sure you include a few 1/8 teaspoons in your survival kit so you'll always have the ability to make this important measurement correctly.

24

USING DRUMS

The next step up in long term water planning is the use of drums. Made of plastic or, less commonly – steel, they come in sizes ranging from five gallons all the way up to 55 gallons or more.

There are many sources online for purchasing drums to store water in, just make sure you get drums that are certified as "food safe". Only drums with this certification are suitable for the safe storage of water. Regular drums, even if brand new, could have manufacturing residue inside, not to mention bacteria or other pathogens that would contaminate your water.

Plastic drums are recommended not only because they're easier to find and usually cheaper, they are not vulnerable to corrosion like metal drums are. They also weigh less when empty, making them easier to move when empty. When purchasing drums for your survival kit, make sure you obtain all the associated hardware you'll need for working with them.

You'll need a device called a "bung wrench", an inexpensive, but vital tool. It allows you to tighten or remove the lids on your drums. There are two ways to store your drums: Upright or on their sides. If you pick the sideways option, you'll need a drum rack. These are shelf like structures that "cradle" the drum, keeping it off the floor and stable. Drums have the advantage of being stackable, allowing you to store a larger volume of water in a smaller space. This method will also require you to purchase valves that screw into the openings in the drums in order to dispense the water. Ensure again that all these accessories are certified food-safe. One final item to keep in mind is weight. A 55 gallon drum weighs several hundred pounds; once filled you won't be able to budge it. If using a rack, make sure to mount your drums before you fill them. If you're stacking, keep the total weight in mind and make sure the floor where you place it can handle the stress. Multiple drums of water can be measured in tons.

If you store your drums upright, you'll be less space-efficient; but you won't have to go to the trouble and expense of purchasing drum racks. However, you will need a pump to get the water from the drum. This is another device for which several brands and varieties are available – again, look first for the food safe certification. Although more expensive, try to get a brand that is made of stainless steel. Do not buy an electric pump; only a manually operated one. You can guess why.

Since you won't be purchasing drums pre-filled with treated water, you'll likely fill them yourself. Just like with smaller bottles, you can use plain, unscented household bleach. Check online for the proper ratios for your volume of container, but for convenience, think a full teaspoon for five gallon buckets; 5 ½ teaspoons for fifty-five gallon drums. There are also commercial products specifically designed to purify water as well, but regular bleach is comparably effective making the additional expense unnecessary.

In anticipation of very long-term disasters, water tanks with larger volumes are an option to consider. Expensive to buy and install, these tanks can hold anywhere from a few hundred to several thousand gallons. A fine solution to long-term water needs, I prefer several, smaller containers. First, if you should have to evacuate your shelter (quite possible), all that time and investment is wasted. Second, if your water supply becomes contaminated, it's all contaminated. It's your one, single water supply. If you have your water dispersed amongst multiple containers, and one becomes contaminated or spills, you still have plenty remaining.

Just to quickly mention, you can always boil your water. If you have to resort to this, fine, but try to avoid it if you can. Boiling water uses precious resources and is of course noticeable. Purification can be done safely with iodine as well, but since iodine isn't commonly available any more, I will not recommend its usage.

You will note that the water storage ideas mentioned here focused mostly on the premise of a permanent shelter. We will now talk about other water solutions in the next section.

BUGGING
OUT

CHAPTER FOUR
BUGGING OUT

Leaving. Hittin' the road. In the first section, we repeatedly stressed the importance of preparation. Preparation becomes no less important in this section, but an issue that will be considered of equal importance is portability.

Weight, bulk, and how quickly you can pack and prepare to move again - these are the main components of portability. Preparing a portable survival kit is just as important, if not more so, than preparation of your shelter. You can only use your shelter supplies at your shelter, whereas you can use your portable survival kit anywhere.

When planning your bug-out kit, the same principles apply; food, water and shelter. Security as well. All the supplies you bring must be subject to the over-arching need for portability. Consider this: to survive, let's say you need a pound of food a day, (this is highly subject to what kind of food, level of activity, the person's size and metabolism, but for sake of example...) and a gallon of water. The water weighs eight pounds just by itself.

Now, if we wanted to carry five day's worth of supplies, that's 45 pounds right there. And we haven't even considered the weight of the containers for the food and water, the utensils for cooking and/ or eating. What about the weight of a tent? Tools like a shovel? A gun and ammunition for protection? Your backpack and even the weight of your clothes need to be added in.

You can see, that for just five days of supplies, we are already hauling around almost a hundred pounds. Even for the strongest, this is far too much weight. See for yourself if you wish. Get a backpack, and put a mere 30 or so pounds of weight in it, then go hike some trails at your local park for an hour or two. Unless you're in peak physical condition, you will see just how fatiguing this can be. You will see that thirty pounds may not seem like much, but it gets a lot heavier after you carry it around for a few hours. Not only does excess weight tire you out and slow you down, but you'll require extra food to burn all those calories. You'll also need extra water to replace what you sweat out.

When we think about a survival kit for traveling, we won't carry much in the way of consumable stores. What we will carry are mostly the tools to obtain a constant supply of the things we need. Let's begin.

25

THE BACKPACK

Although you could carry your survival supplies around in a suitcase, a backpack is certainly preferable. By carrying your supplies around on your back, the weight is better distributed on your frame, allowing you to carry more. Carrying even a very lightweight bag in your arms will tire you out after only a very short time. Which leads to the other advantage; a backpack leaves your arms and hands free. Climbing, using maps, compasses and tools all can be done much more easily and quickly if your hands are unburdened by supplies.

Also, for the issue of security, if you're carrying a weapon, you'll likely need it in a hurry. Having your hands constantly free promotes the ability to defend yourself at short notice.

When selecting a backpack, get the best your budget can afford. Look for one constructed out of lightweight nylon (for strength, durability and water resistance) and an aluminum frame. Having a frame will allow the pack to set more comfortably on your body even when heavily loaded and it also provides some structure to your pack. This helps to keep items from being crushed or containers bursting if you need to set your pack down. Look for one that features an exterior shelf on the frame for carrying a tent. This will allow you to roll up and carry your tent while it's still wet without significant problems.

Look for a backpack that has multiple compartments. Not only will this help you keep track of your supplies and facilitate easier packing and unpacking, but can help isolate messes. For example, if you have a bottle of water stored in the main compartment of your pack, and it leaks, the bulk of your supplies are now soaked. A serious inconvenience in a mild climate; a dangerous situation in a climate cold enough for water to freeze.

When selecting a pack, try on several different ones to find the one most comfortable for you. Try to focus your search on a pack that has wide, well-padded shoulder straps. This is the part of your body that bears the majority of the weight. After walking for an extended time, the straps will begin to dig into your shoulders. Wider straps distribute more of the weight, and so will be less uncomfortable over time.

Some excellent packs can be sourced from REI.com, I have had good experience with their REI Mars 80 pack, which has lasted an exceptionally long time, is very durable and easy to wear. A lot of people swear by packs with metal frames, but it's important to make sure that whatever pack you choose, it will suit your body type, and can be comfortably worn for hours, if not days when fully packed.

After you select your pack and take it home, assemble your likely supplies and pack and re-pack them. Not only to see how best to arrange your supplies in the most space-efficient manner possible, but also for the practice. You never know when you might have to pack up and leave in a hurry, so by practicing this important skill, you will be ready if and when the time arrives.

If you have young children or babies, there are 'packs' or carriers specifically designed for wearing them and are excellent for everyday use, as well as during emergencies - a time that you will need your hands free. If this is something needed by your family, be sure to do your research on the features of each carrier, i.e.: their weight capacity, durability and proper hip positioning. If you will be wearing your baby or small child for a long duration, you want your carrier to properly support their spine and hips. Some excellent choices are an ERGO or BECO baby carrier, or a cloth ring sling for younger ones which supports their physical development and also allows them to be kept safe and close to you. A ring sling also allows you to wear them in a variety of positions, including the back, side and front.

If you are forced to use your pack in an emergency situation, make sure that you completely unpack it and let it air out every few days. Any trapped moisture, especially from when your back sweats, will encourage the growth of mold and bacteria. This is not only a health risk (as it could contaminate food or water supplies and cooking and eating utensils), but mould will significantly weaken the material in your pack. Take good care of your backpack, as you're not likely to find a new one to replace it should yours become damaged. Now, as in the previous section, let us examine the basics of survival.

26

SHELTER

Standard items for shelter in our kit would be a tent and sleeping bag. Depending on types, this can be as much as twenty pounds. The only way to go lighter with these items is to spend more money. Your basic considerations are similar to those for your backpack: Nylon tent for it's environmental resistance and light weight. A compact, lightweight sleeping bag of similar construction. If you anticipate traveling with people besides yourself, such as your family, you might want to get a tent large enough for all of you.

However, I would suggest that you buy multiple smaller tents for each member of your party. First, because rather than have one person carry the additional weight and bulk of a larger tent, you'll be spreading the weight around instead. Also, what if your tent becomes damaged or destroyed? If you only have the one tent, you're out of luck. But with multiple tents, you at least have the option of sharing if you need to, even if the space is a little crowded.

If your budget doesn't permit the purchase of a tent, or you're just looking to minimize the weight and bulk in your pack, a simple plastic tarp and some rope is a much less suitable, but still usable option. As mentioned earlier, get a plastic tarp for rain and snow resistance, and nylon rope for water and rot resistance.

Obviously, one of the main drawbacks compared to a tent is the inability to completely seal out the elements, especially the cold. When using the tarp and rope for shelter, you would customarily secure the rope to two solid points, and drape the tarp over the top. As you can imagine with this setup, you're really only protected from rain or snow. Your "tent" is still open on both sides.

Suffice it to say, if your budget allows it, get the tent and accept the penalty of the added weight. Although, carrying it around will cause additional fatigue, not getting adequate sleep because you're cold, or even worse, risking illness makes the added weight worthwhile.

One thing that could make the non-tent option of greater utility is if you live in an urban area. This line of thinking carries with it it's own risks, of course, but if you can reliably and consistently set up shelter in an abandoned building or similar structure, then a tarp and rope combo become sufficient. But again, you really have no way of knowing if such preexisting structures will be available, so in the end, it's still better if you invest in a good tent.

As I said, you can't predict if preexisting structures will be available in a disaster. That wisdom cuts both ways; you don't know that they won't be available either. Therefore, you should carry some supplies should you come across such a find. A hammer is a good tool in this situation, but in the interest of efficiency, a hatchet with a hammer head on it is the ideal choice. The hatchet (ax) is obvious - a tool basic to a portable survival kit. You'll hopefully have one or more flashlights. Abandoned buildings are notoriously dark inside. In the next section we'll talk about the types of things to carry besides food, water and shelter.

The last major option you can prepare for is living underground. This should only be considered practical as a last resort and if you have time, security and plenty of energy. In order to dig even a small burrow, just large enough to lay in, you will be required to excavate several tons of dirt. But it's possible that circumstances could leave you with no other choice, so it's worthwhile to prepare for it. While the act might be taxing, preparing for it is quite easy. All you need is a shovel. For the sake of portability, try to get one in the same style as that carried by infantry in the army; a small, folding shovel.

I've given a few reasons why going underground should be considered a last resort, and here is the most important one: It can be dangerous. Being buried alive is a fear shared by most people. And getting buried alive can happen very easily when digging underground. Minimize this risk; don't dig a tunnel to deeply - in the event of a cave in, you'll have a much better chance of escape if there are a few hundred pounds of soil on top of you instead of a few tons. Don't dig in sandy or unstable soil. This is just asking to be buried in a cave-in. In short, don't make an underground shelter unless you have no other alternative.

Finally, when traveling, always be on the lookout for a place where you can stay, if not indefinitely, then at least for a very long time. Having a permanent shelter is much less taxing, more secure and affords you far greater options to survive. Such as growing your food and being able to store a larger amount of supplies, for example.

27

FOOD

At least a pound a day. Seven pounds a week. Thirty for a whole month. Carrying adequate supplies of food is difficult at best, and impossible at worst. Who knows how long a disaster will last. Therefore, you need to have the ability to acquire it when your supplies inevitably run out.

That isn't to say that you shouldn't carry at least some food. After all, It's quite likely you'll be in situations where there simply is no food to obtain, so you'll have to have something to keep up your energy during these times (or, to keep you from starving).

Since there are many different types of food we can carry that will satisfy our nutritional needs, our primary focus should be portability. That means foods that are lightweight, nutritionally dense and easy to prepare. As mentioned, Energy bars mostly fulfill this role, but the sugar content and absence of many vital nutrients make this a rather undesirable choice. The cost is rather high as well.

Canned goods aren't really a good choice from a weight standpoint, unless we're talking about freeze-dried foods. However, the weight savings might be offset by the need for additional water to reconstitute the freeze-dried supplies (typically, these come in a can, but some are packed in Mylar pouches). If your budget is reasonable, camping supply stores have a wide selection of foods suitable for survival. After all, traveling in a survival situation can essentially be thought of as one, long camping trip.

As usual, some of the best solutions are also the most cost-effective. For bulk energy, oatmeal is an ideal choice. Very light and space efficient, it requires only a small amount of water to make and can also be eaten cold. A few pounds of oatmeal along with a vial of multivitamins and you can survive for weeks; perhaps even months if you ration carefully. Oatmeal is a good survival food also because of the way it digests-slowly. It is rich in carbohydrates for energy. Unless you cannot stand to eat oatmeal, I strongly recommend you make it the core food source of your survival travel kit.

A few more words about vitamins and the importance of getting enough: As I keep repeating, survival in an emergency situation is likely to be a very stressful affair. This is going to take a heavy toll on your immune system. If you're traveling, constant exposure to the elements is certainly going to test your health also.

As you know, proper function of your immune system is heavily dependent on getting enough of the right vitamins. Vitamins C, A, E and the B vitamins are some of the nutrients your immune system must have (and in sufficient quantities) to function. Remember: There isn't any medical care available. No Penicillin, no antibiotics. If you catch a cold, get a little cut on your finger; it's no longer a minor little thing. It can very easily become a serious, life-threatening issue.

If you catch a cold - especially if you don't have warm, dry shelter, your minor little cold can easily develop into bronchitis. Bronchitis can easily develop into pneumonia. You know what can happen next. A tiny little cut can easily become infected. Especially when you consider both the unsanitary conditions you're likely to face when traveling and the unlikely access to soap and water to clean your cut off. Untreated infections can quickly turn gangrenous, and if that happens you will die without professional medical attention.

Bottom line: ALWAYS carry multivitamins in your traveling survival kit.

28

PLANTS, BERRIES & MUSHROOMS

Unless you were raised pretty much from birth in the wilderness, the first thing you'll want to get for your traveling survival kit is a book on edible plants, berries and mushrooms.

There are several thousands of different plants and mushrooms that are healthy and safe to eat in the wild. Likewise, there are many that aren't so edible. Ranging from things that might upset your stomach, to those that could kill you in minutes, you must be able to accurately and consistently identify which ones are safe to eat. Since there are so many different plants, berries and mushrooms that vary from area to area, a comprehensive book is your best approach.

There are many books available on this topic, so try to select one that is appropriate to your general area and climate. Get one that is small and with a soft cover so as to facilitate easy packing. Also, try to get one with laminated (plastic coated) pages. A good, visual clue as to whether or not a book has laminated pages is that it has a spiral binding - good to know if you're shopping online and can't actually examine the book in your own hands. It's likely your book will get wet, and so having laminated pages will keep it from being ruined. They're also easier to clean, as it's likely you'll be using your book in muddy areas and you'll frequently have dirty hands when you're traveling. Finally, make sure your book uses color photographs to illustrate the plans, especially mushrooms. Some plants, (like mushrooms) have species that might look somewhat similar, but are actually not. And that difference could be a high volume of poison. Only color photographs can help you to really be sure if a plant is the one you think it is or not.

29

HUNTING GEAR

Although you might have reservations due to your feelings about guns, or animal rights, it must be acknowledged that circumstances could force you to rely on game for food. This being the case, you should prepare for this possibility. When it comes to hunting, we can divide it into three different classifications: Hunting with a gun, hunting with a bow and trapping.

Hunting with a gun: This is one of those topics that is too broad to be covered in these pages, but some points to keep in mind: firearms, particularly rifles, are a good choice for hunting. True, however, between the actual gun, ammunition and cleaning supplies, we're talking about a large amount of weight. But consider this; hunting with a firearm is the easiest to learn and do. Compared to the other methods, it offers the best chance that you will actually obtain the food you're after, rather than it getting away.

We'll talk more about security later, but this is the other advantage to firearms. Personal security. Being a refugee in an emergency is dangerous business. You will likely have to watch out for dangerous animals like feral dogs and other refugees who are without supplies and who will gladly take yours. There are no police or sheriffs. It's likely that merely being seen with a gun will be enough to discourage most bandits. In the end, should worse come to worse, possessing a gun has the dual benefit of both security and the ability to effectively hunt, and so should therefore be seriously considered as part of your survival kit.

Hunting with a bow: Compared to hunting with a gun, a bow weapon (longbow or crossbow) has a few advantages and drawbacks. Keeping a low profile during a catastrophe is the best course of action, but if you fire a gun, you're making noise that can be heard for miles. Bow weapons are virtually silent. No one nearby will be alerted to your presence when you use a bow. Arrows – your ammunition, can be reused, unlike the bullets for a gun.

The drawbacks to bow hunting are pretty serious though. Hunting with a bow takes a great deal of skill, and no matter how skillful you are, hunting smaller game like rabbits and squirrels is difficult almost to the point of impossibility. Since this is the type of game you are most likely to encounter, bow hunting might not be your best option. One more negative point to consider is that while fairly light, bow hunting equipment is bulky and not so easily carried or concealed.

Trapping: Some might be opposed to this method for humane reasons, but while there are drawbacks here as well, this method is useful enough to bear mention. Trapping can be an effective method for getting small game - the process allows you to go off and perform other tasks after the trap is set. If you have the ability to set multiple traps, this can significantly increase your chances of success.

A successful trap setting requires a moderate amount of skill. It also restricts your mobility, as you must remain in the general area of your traps to check them and harvest any food they catch. If circumstances force you to flee an area, you'll be leaving your traps behind. Since it's more likely that other refugees will be out foraging for food, another person could become ensnared by one of your traps, leading to a dangerous confrontation.

Lastly, you'll need a few more tools to prepare your game after you've bagged it: A good quality hunting knife to skin and prepare your food, proper utensils like a pan to cook with and a fork to make it easier to eat. A camping supply store or the internet are good places to find a camp cook kit. Carry an airtight container and a good quantity of salt so you can preserve and store what you don't eat right away for later (preserving meats is another comprehensive topic you'll need to research further).

Each one of these hunting methods has both its advantages and disadvantages. Hunting with a firearm is the best choice for the majority of people, but you'll have to think and prepare on which method you think is best for your particular circumstances and objectives.

30

FISHING SUPPLIES

If I remember correctly, something like 80% of the Earth's surface is covered with water. This makes it pretty likely that if you're out traveling in a survival situation, you'll come across a lake or a stream that has fish to eat. High in protein, able to be eaten raw if you have to (but certainly not very pleasant) and fairly easy to prepare for, fishing gear is a very important component of your survival kit. Again, camping, sporting goods stores and the internet are good places to buy fishing gear, but orient your purchases with one of our most important objectives: Portability.

There are many different brands of portable fishing rods, try to get one made of durable materials that is simple in construction. The simpler the device, the less things can go wrong with it. There are several that can be disassembled and fitted into their own case, allowing you to carry ancillary supplies as well. Fishing equipment is relatively inexpensive, but if you need or want to go cheap, you can. Some fishing line, hooks, bobbers, weights and maybe some lures can be purchased separately for you to make your own fishing kit. Fishing without a rod is more difficult, but this method has the advantage of taking up very little space. It shouldn't be too difficult to gather worms or bugs to use as bait. Speaking of which...

Worms and Bugs. There isn't a whole lot to explain here really. If things get really bad, and you have no other alternative, you can always eat insects - and that's pretty much it. Other than considerations of taste, you don't really have to be selective. You should avoid common flies and related bugs as you don't know if they've been into feces, which could make you ill. Aside from that, your choices are wide open. Yum!

31

WATER

Water. The one thing you cannot survive for long without. As we've established, water is rather heavy, so carrying an adequate quantity can be difficult. None the less, seeing how it also might be at times difficult to find while traveling, we should always carry as much as we can.

The best method for carrying water is in a stainless steel canteen or bottle. Durable, rustproof, stainless steel is also very difficult to crush. This is why you should avoid plastic bottles. Packed incorrectly, or if you set your pack down the wrong way, you could put crushing weight on a plastic bottle causing it to burst. Now, not only are you short a water container, but many of your supplies might be soaked as well. Some items, such as a radio or flashlight could be ruined forever if packed in the same compartment where the spill took place. Although they weigh and cost slightly more, stainless steel containers are worth the trouble.

Still, no matter how much water you carry or how you carry it, you'll soon run out and will need more. This means getting water that is potentially unsafe to drink. We talked about how you can easily and inexpensively use regular household bleach to purify your drinking supplies, and that advice will work well here as well. But there are a few differences.

When we talked about sanitizing water before, we were talking about water that was relatively clear and free of pollutants - we were mainly concerned with bacteria and associated water-born illnesses. However, in the wild, your water sources could be lakes, streams, ponds and even puddles. Not only do we need to worry about bacteria, but dirt, fungus, animal waste and microorganisms will be present as well. As I mentioned previously, there are portable water purifying products like the life straw or the lifesaver bottle that would be an invaluable tool in a situation like this. If, however, you don't have a device like this, it is important that prior to sanitizing your water, you clean it as best you can. There are several ways to do this. One way, if the surface of your water source is clean, is to skim the water off the surface. Submerge your container so the opening is just beneath the surface. Allow the water to flow into the container slowly, so as not to stir up additional sediment. You can filter your water by pouring it into a crude paper or cloth filter. Budget permitting, there are several filter products designed for camping that are portable and reusable. Some of the more expensive, higher quality brands have filters that are so advanced, they can even filter out bacteria. If you can, you should really invest in a filter of this nature.

Next, after proper filtration, we'll need to sanitize our water. You can use bleach, and that's fine, but for obtaining water in the wild, there's a better solution you should consider: Water Purification Tablets. Bleach is a very effective purification method, but it won't kill every organism that contaminates water. The kind of water you'll be encountering whilst traveling is more likely to have these exotic pathogens. Water purification tablets are specifically formulated to purify water for drinking (probably why they have that name). You fill up your water container, drop one of these tablets in, and forget about it.

When searching for water, keep in mind that some water cannot be easily made safe to drink. If you are traveling in an urban area, avoid any water that is near to industrial or manufacturing facilities. If you're out in a rural area, stay away from water around gas and oil wells or pipelines. Be careful of water around farms - it could be contaminated with animal waste (treatable) or fertilizer runoff (not easily treatable).

There are a couple of less desirable methods for water purification: boiling, (not preferable for the energy it uses and the attention it can draw) Iodine (a scarce product) and sunlight. You can put relatively clean water into clear plastic bottles and leave it set in the sun for a few hours. Ultraviolet rays destroy bacteria and mold just as effectively as chemicals. The downside to using plastic bottles however, is that placing them in the sun has been found to leach the chemical Dioxin into the water. A better option (should you have them) would be to use glass bottles, or a mason jar instead. Bottles must be placed on a white surface and turned regularly to make sure all the water is fully exposed to the UV rays. This process is useful, but requires packing heavier glass bottles in your kit, and a white reflective surface that is likely to be noticeable from quite a ways away.

32

RAIN COLLECTION

Even if you have selected a tent as your traveling shelter, a plastic tarp still has many uses - collecting rainwater being the main one. It's easy. Spread out your tarp horizontally, with a slight incline that funnels into a water container. Just make sure your tarp is clean before you do this to save the trouble of filtering your water before you can drink it. Just remember, (this is true for snowmelt as well), that this water is like distilled water; devoid of minerals. Long-term consumption will deplete your body of vital minerals. Please note that if you are ever in a position where the only water source you have is from snow, you should never eat it directly. Yes the snow will turn to liquid when you eat it, but it will rob your body of precious heat. Eating snow requires much more energy from your body to convert the snow to usable water than the energy your body will actually get out of it. Instead, it is best to stuff the snow into a container and put it between layers of your clothing (not directly against your skin). Doing this will allow your radiant body heat to melt it, without directly taking heat from you.

33

SOLAR STILL

Sometimes, you might find yourself in an area where no source of water exists (hopefully it is not an area as extreme as, say, a desert - although water can still be sourced in such an environment). Keep this little rule of thumb in mind: If there's vegetation, there's water. This is a very important tip, so make sure you learn it well. You can get water from a Solar Still. The supplies you will need are a piece of heavier gauge plastic at least a square foot or slightly larger (preferably clear). A container for water and some rocks. First, you dig a hole about 8 to 12 inches deep (20 to 30 centimeters) and place your water container at the bottom in the center. Collect some leaves and assorted moist vegetation, chop it up and spread it around the bottom of the hole surrounding the container. Loosely lay the plastic over the top of the hole, and secure it by placing rocks around the edges. Place a small stone directly in the center of the plastic, so that it weighs down the center, forming an inverted cone (the point of which is directly over the opening of your water container). As the sun heats up the vegetation, water will evaporate and condense on the underside of your plastic sheet. As more moisture collects, drops will form that will run down the plastic and into your cup.

This is a sure-fire method of collecting water when the conditions are right (when there is sunlight and it's not too cold outside) but it can be somewhat time consuming. Since the materials for collecting water in this way are cheap, light and take up little space, you can construct multiple stills to collect more water even faster.

Given the importance of this particular information, I have included a small illustration to show its construction so there won't be any confusion or ambiguity. I'm not an artist, so please forgive its crudity, but it does clearly show how it's done:

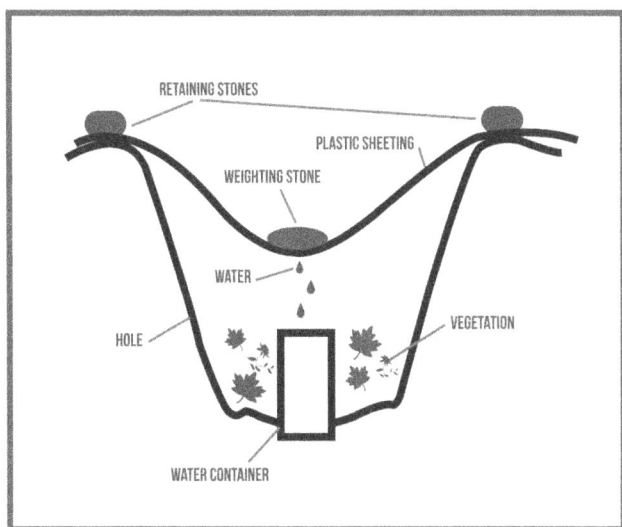

Just take care when removing the plastic so that dirt, debris or even your weighting stone don't fall into your water.

Lastly, there is the option of digging for water. I only mention this to remind you that you can. Don't depend upon it. The ability to get water by digging is an iffy proposition at best. Unless you really know what you're doing, you could end up wasting a lot of time and energy for no result.

MISCELLANEOUS

CHAPTER FIVE

MISCELLANEOUS

ALTHOUGH THIS FINAL SECTION IS ENTITLED "MISCELLANEOUS", please don't take it to mean that the following information is any less important than that contained in the first two sections. These tips are here because they either apply to both shelter survival and travel survival with equal importance or they do not fit easily into one of those categories.

34

SHOES

We used this as an example in the beginning of this book. Hopefully, it made you think about the importance of this often overlooked aspect of survival preparation. As you might have guessed, my first recommendation is for you to obtain a good pair of hiking boots. Factors to prioritize are comfort, durability and water resistance. Such shoes will not be cheap, but good, long-wearing footwear is absolutely essential in any survival scenario. Once you've purchased these boots, go and buy another pair. Or two. Bottom line, buy as many as you can possibly afford because, as I keep preaching, you probably won't be able to find more after a catastrophe gets under way. Shoes are something that you absolutely must have and yet, wear out regularly. Stock up with as many as you can. Once you purchase your shoes, take a long walk with them to break them in. If, after your boots are broken in, they are uncomfortable or give you blisters after awhile, discard them and try a different brand. Blisters are not only uncomfortable, but can become infected.

Unless you live in a climate that is perpetually cold, get as many pairs of hiking sandals as you can as well. When we walk, our feet sweat. When we walk long distances for long periods of time, this sweat promotes the growth of bacteria on our feet. Many long distance hikers (climate permitting) eschew boots for sandals due to the superior ventilation sandals provide. A case of athlete's foot in normal times is a minor inconvenience; foot fungus in a survival situation can easily turn into a serious problem.

35

SOCKS

Along with good shoes, socks are a very important part of your survival kit. Make sure you have numerous pairs of good quality white cotton socks. White socks tend to be less prone to fungal growth. Cotton is comfortable and good at absorbing sweat, as is wool, which wicks moisture away from your body. Wool is warm, breathable, naturally antifungal, antibacterial and doesn't smell after prolonged usage. Be sure to launder and thoroughly dry your socks often to kill any bacteria that might be growing. When walking long distances or for long periods, stop, remove your shoes and change your socks. After a while, as your feet sweat, not only can bacteria start to grow, but wet socks will abrade your skin inside your boots. This not only makes walking uncomfortable, it slows you down and can become a threat of further infection.

36

CLOTHING

Warm, light, durable and long lasting. These are the principle considerations in choosing proper clothes for survival. Jeans, not designer, but work pants. Focus on clothing designed for camping or outdoor work. Choose cotton for the articles that touch your skin, and waterproof canvas or nylon for outerwear. High tech materials or wool, like the kind that wick away sweat are also ideal choices next to your skin, but cost more. When it's warm and sunny, dress light with your exposed skin covered to protect from sunburn. Wearing a hat is also a good idea.

A hat (different kind) should also be worn when it's cold. Just like Mom said, you lose most of your body heat through your head. For the colder climates, a good, waterproof coat with polyester fill is adequate, but you should consider dressing in layers. Layers will keep you just as warm if not warmer, and have the advantage of allowing you to shed or add layers to adjust yourself to a comfortable temperature. If your layers get wet, they can be separated to dry more quickly than a heavier coat. If your coat becomes damaged or frayed, then you're without proper protection. If one of your layers become unusable, you still have others to provide at least some warmth. Always try to avoid placing all of your eggs in one basket (when possible).

37

BATHING & SANITATION

Being clean is not just important to your morale during a crisis, it's a health threat when you don't do it regularly. Taking a shower or a bath isn't really feasible in an emergency, especially if you're traveling. Still, there are steps you can take and a minimal amount of supplies you can carry for performing this vital task. You can carry regular soap, which doesn't weigh much - but this option requires access to water which may be limited. In spite of this drawback, make sure you include soap in your survival kit. You might not be able to use it often, but bathing with soap and water is really the only way to clean dirt and skin oil.

Carry a bottle of isopropyl (rubbing) alcohol or Listerine. These are acceptable alternatives to soap, and have other advantages as well, in that they kill bacteria but don't require water to do it. At least twice a day (morning and before you go to bed), soak a towel or rag with some rubbing alcohol and rub it on your feet, under your armpits, or anywhere you have skin to skin contact and sweat, such as your waistline. This includes your lower extremities, but be careful - you'll want to dilute the alcohol otherwise it will likely "burn" in this sensitive area.

When it comes to shaving, don't do it (this applies to men's faces as well as ladies' underarms and legs). First, the additional body hair insulates you from cold and can protect your skin from injury. The biggest drawback with shaving, is that it creates little "microcuts" on your skin (this is why your skin sometimes feels raw and irritated after you shave). These little cuts, not to mention actual, full size nicks, are avenues for infection. A negligible annoyance usually, it can become a potentially life-threatening situation during a crisis.

You need to pay special attention to your oral health as well. This is another task that is best performed with water, but you can get by if you must. Pack a few toothbrushes (because this item is difficult to replace or substitute), floss and toothpaste in your kit. After all, brushing your teeth really doesn't require very much water. Even if you can't brush the traditional way, with water, the brushing and flossing will dislodge the majority of the food particles. Just make sure you spit it all out when you're done. Some alternatives to toothpaste should you run out, is baking soda, salt and natural clay.

Look after your oral health. I hate to beat a dead horse, but dental problems can become serious, and without professional dental care – they can become deadly. Take the proper precautions by brushing and flossing every time after you eat, when you wake up and before you go to bed. Some of your oral health supplies are beneficial due to their "dual use" ability. Rubbing alcohol can be used to disinfect cuts and be burned in an alcohol stove. Listerine can both disinfect cuts and be used as a mouthwash. Anytime you can carry a single item that serves more than one distinct purpose, seriously consider doing so.

Whether you're in a permanent shelter or traveling, you'll need to use the restroom many times during the day. Since there probably aren't any restrooms available, we'll have to make our own. Other than a shovel, no special equipment is needed. For a permanent or semi-permanent shelter, just dig a latrine (hole or trench) about two or three feet (60 cm to 1m) deep. Make sure you dig your latrine away from your shelter, because of the smell and bugs. Take care not to place a latrine near any existing or potential future water supplies (fecal contamination is the cause of many water-born illnesses). For the sake of comfort, you can cut a hole in a sturdy box or crate and place it over your latrine to sit on while you do your business. If a box isn't available, you can mount a log or thick branch over your latrine to sit on bench-style. When you latrine gets excessively bad smelling, or is about 1/8 to ¼ full, fill it over with clean dirt and dig a new one.

When traveling, digging a shallow hole for your waste is adequate. Just follow the same guidelines with regards to nearby water supplies. Make sure you bury your waste. You don't want to leave evidence of your presence for other people or even possible predatory animals.

Obviously, toilet paper is going to be hard to come by - even if you've stocked up, you'll still run out during a long-term crisis. Whereas you could stock up on cloths for this function, and wash and reuse them, this isn't easy with a permanent shelter, and is downright difficult when traveling. Using cloths is also risky due to the unsanitary practice of handling raw feces when you clean them. You may find yourself resorting to the age-old practice of using leaves.

Select the leaves you'll use for this purpose carefully. I don't just mean avoiding poison ivy and the like, but try to select leaves that are soft, wide, not too "veiny" and won't tear easily. Remove any stems. The reason for this isn't just comfort (although that's important too), it's because your nether regions are delicate. You can very easily tear or abrade your skin down there, making it uncomfortable to walk, and you could be opening a path to infection. Make sure you're prepared - in advance - by gathering more leaves than you think you'll need. You'll be using these things by the handful, and will go through them fast. Try not to get anything on your hands - wipe them clean if you do. Wash with soap and water or rinse with alcohol when you're done.

One final preparation to make in this category (if you're a woman) is menstrual needs. Your local drugstore may or may not stock them, but there are numerous brands of reusable tampons on the internet. Simply use the search terms "reusable" or "eco-friendly" tampons, cloth pads or menstrual cups, and you'll have several varieties from which to choose.

38

MEDICATION

Mostly, we're talking about over-the-counter type substances here. If you require regular prescriptions for a health issue, you'll have to do your personal best in securing enough to last you in an emergency. The nature of prescription medication can severely restrict your ability to do this.

What we're concerned with are things like painkillers, antihistamines, antacids and the like. A headache or hay fever may seem like small things in the face of a disaster, but it's little things like this that can make you tire more quickly. They interfere with your concentration, making you less aware of what's happening around you. Having an upset stomach can do the same and can result in vomiting, which will rapidly dehydrate you.

Painkillers such as Tylenol and Advil can be useful in treating aches and pains from extended walking or labor. Moderate to severe muscle soreness can slow you down or make sleep difficult. You can expect that even if you're careful, you'll still get minor injuries for which some temporary pain relief might be useful and welcome. It's also expected that you could get sick with a virus from time to time. Tylenol is good for helping reduce fever, however it is important to note that fevers are actually beneficial to the body - they are the body's defense against infection, and fevers up to 106 are considered safe, barring head injury. Some other items you might want to consider having on hand as alternatives to conventional medication is essential oils. Things like peppermint essential oil is excellent for headaches (as is peppermint tea), and is also good for muscle pain or nausea/vomiting. Other essential oils such as thyme is naturally antibacterial, and oil of oregano is good for food poisoning. These oils are in bottles that are very small and easily portable.

When it comes to illness, there are two herbs you should include in your survival pack. Echinacea and oil of oregano. Echinacea is the brand name of an over-the-counter cold treatment. If you're not already familiar with it, it comes in tincture form, dried form (for teas, or homemade capsules) and capsule form. Get the tincture form, preferably alcohol based. Most importantly, this variety (as long as it is well prepared) has NO expiration date, even though they may include one on the bottle. If kept in a cool dark place, it will last indefinitely. The glycerine-based one is not as effective, so if you do not like the alcohol taste, simply boil some water and drop some droplets into it then wait a few minutes for the alcohol to dissipate before consuming. When you feel the onset of a cold, take this tincture - it will help lessen the severity of your cold, or help cure it altogether. Echinacea contains nutrients and vitamins specifically designed to boost your immune system. It really does work. I've used it for years, and many of my peers have reported similar, positive results. I usually mega dose for the first three days (2-3 droppers full, 2-3 times a day), and then go down to a regular dosage for up to three days more should I need it. It is important to stop for one day (the seventh day) before continuing (should you need it), so that it continues to be effective. I have used this successfully with my family, my wife has used it for mastitis, and it is even gentle enough to use with children. It is safe during pregnancy, breastfeeding and for little ones. It is also very cheap, so it's a good idea to stock up on as many bottles as you can.

You should do everything in your power to avoid getting sick. If (when) you do, you should take very good care of yourself - not only to get better, but so you don't get worse. Lots of people succumb to illness during crises, but the initial cold or infection isn't what got them. Usually, they fall victim to a secondary infection. Being ill burdens and weakens your immune system. In this weakened state, it's much easier to become afflicted with something much more serious than a cold or flu.

The flu virus, like the cold virus and every other virus, is incurable. The only known cure for any virus to date is your own immune system. Taking echinacea and natural vitamin C (like that found in acerola berries, rose hips and oranges) helps strengthen your immune system so that it can defeat the cold virus. Until recently, aside from vaccination, there was no treatment for flu. In recent years, two drugs have been developed that successfully treat the flu: Tamiflu and Relenza. I won't go into the chemistry (even if we had space, it's over most people's head's - including mine), but I don't feel that vaccination or medications such as these are an effective treatment against the flu, especially in a crisis situation. The reason is that strains of flu are constantly changing, and by the time chemists develop a vaccination by using the previous year's strain, it has already changed form in the general population. Secondly, both of these medicines are only available with a prescription and are not cheap. Should there be no access to medical care during a crisis, these drugs would be unattainable anyways.

I am a firm believer in maintaining health through diet and exercise as a preventative measure so that your body is in its best position to be able to fight off illness, should it need to. Taking herbs or medications that aid the body in fighting, are a much better choice in my opinion than succumbing to toxic alternatives. The second herb that I would not be without is oil of oregano. I use this primarily in cases of food poisoning, or any other type of viral or bacterial illness. It's strong in taste, but very effective.

39

FIRST AID

You're on your own and injuries, some serious, are almost inevitable. You'll need both tools and skill for this. The best preparation is to take a course in comprehensive first aid if you can. If not, get a first-aid book along the same lines as your plant and mushroom book; small, full of color pictures and laminated.

You can buy a first aid kit at your local drugstore, but the best survival first aid kit is the one you build yourself. Get a sturdy, water-tight box, large enough for the following items:

- Band-aids and bandages
- Ointments or lotions for bug bites or plant rashes
- Antiseptic ointment like Neosporin
- Pourable antiseptic like Listerine
- Alcohol or hydrogen peroxide
- Gauze pads and cotton swabs for cleaning out deeper wounds
- An eyewash attachment for one of your water containers (in case you get something splashed in your eyes – this is especially important for your permanent shelter kit also if you have a home generator that's diesel fueled)
- Splints for fingers, larger splints for arms and legs (you'll likely carry the larger ones outside the first-aid box)
- Scissors like the kind used by paramedics or nurses known as "lister scissors"
- Tweezers and needles for removing splinters
- Waterproof medical tape
- An instant hand warmer (in case the weather is cold and your hands are too stiff to work)
- Tourniquets
- A suture kit for stitching up severe wounds

If you can't keep drinkable water in your first-aid kit, keep it close at hand. A serious injury with sudden blood loss can cause anything from falling into unconsciousness to dehydration to shock. A sip of water at a time like this can do wonders. Keep your first-aid kit in an easily and readily accessible compartment.

40

DIET & EXERCISE

Right now - I'm not talking post-disaster, I'm talking about your level of physical conditioning before the disaster. I've mentioned repeatedly throughout this guide how stressful a survival situation can be. The amount of strength and stamina required to survive an emergency can be enormous. And once a disaster starts, food is likely to be at a premium, weakening you even further.

If, from day one, from the first moment of a disaster, you have the ability to move quickly and the strength to hike long distances while carrying substantial weight, then you have greatly increased your chances of survival. The initial stages of a crisis are sometimes the most critical. Be prepared by keeping yourself in shape. And make sure your family is in shape as well.

By the way, dying in a natural disaster is little different from dying in a comfortable hospital during normal times from heart disease; you're just as dead either way. Even if you don't anticipate some major disaster, staying in shape all the time is still a pretty good habit to get into. Just sayin'.

41

SAFETY & SECURITY

Desperate times lead to desperate measures. In the event of a survival situation you can modify that slightly to say "Desperate times make for desperate people". I mentioned this earlier: if your kids were starving, what lengths would you go to to feed them? If you said "any", then you're a good parent. There's a lot of good parents out there. And just like you, most of them would kill without hesitation or regret if they felt their families' lives depended on it. You'd probably do the same.

Many readers might be morally opposed to the idea of owning or carrying a gun. In spite of these feelings, a firearm could be the one thing that ends up saving your life. No matter how much food and water you accumulate, no matter how comprehensive your shelter, if someone wants these things and they have a gun (but you don't), then you've just spent a lot of time, effort and money assembling supplies for someone else.

A shotgun or a handgun is most suitable for personal protection. A rifle is better suited for hunting, but is fine for self-defense in most cases. For the sake of weight and supply simplicity (having to stock only one kind of ammo), the rifle is recommended. After all, it's dual use. Good for both hunting and security.
There are many other factors to consider besides just having a gun when it comes to personal security. Getting into a gunfight with some stranger is an iffy and dangerous proposition to begin with; it's better to practice the habits that will help you avoid getting into an altercation in the first place.

If you're residing in your permanent shelter, keep a low profile. Keep quiet and avoid any obvious signs that the place you live in is occupied. If possible, eliminate visual obstructions that prevent you from seeing long distances. Bushes, trees; just make sure you do this before a disaster occurs. During a crisis, don't alter your home or landscaping in ways that are obvious. This includes not repairing any visible damage if you can avoid doing so. Leaks or other damages that will allow further serious damage to your home should be addressed, but anything that would indicate someone is living in your home should be avoided.

If you need to burn a fire, night is the best time. Burning during the day produces a plume of smoke that could be seen many miles away under the right conditions. Burning at night carries this risk as well, since a fire on a dark night could also be seen for miles. The difference is, you can take steps to shroud the visibility of the fire; dig a wide hole, and burn at the bottom, or build your fire in natural depression in the ground. You can't reasonably conceal the smoke from a fire. Either method can be risky, but the risk is slightly less in the dark.

Security when traveling is more important, as you are likely exposed and easier to observe as you go about your business. When traveling, be alert and aware of your surroundings. Stop occasionally and look both close and as far away as you can. The sooner you spot potential trouble, the more time you have to evade or prepare for it. If you have room, carry binoculars so as to see even farther.

When you stop to make shelter in an unfamiliar area (or even in a familiar one), select the area you will make camp and then keep walking past it. Walk a good distance away, then stop and quietly observe the surroundings for a while. Make sure there aren't any strangers around who might approach you without being noticed while your concentration is on setting up your shelter. After you've constructed your shelter, repeat this process to see if anyone is watching you and waiting for you to go to sleep. Unless you have to, don't build a fire, due to the attention it could attract. Be mindful of your food, specifically the smell. There could be other things to worry about besides hungry people. Hungry bears and wolves to name a few.

A small caliber rifle is great for hunting small game, and fine for self-defense, but it is practically worthless against a bear. If you're traveling in an urban area, bears won't concern you much - but if a disaster becomes excessively long-term, bears and other predators will begin showing up anywhere and everywhere. Though it's against common safety regulations, keep your gun loaded and within reach when traveling. If you ever need it in an emergency, you'll likely need it in a hurry.

Safety and security aren't matters solely confined to self-defense against living threats, there are many others. Be slow and cautious if you're crossing difficult terrain. If you have to cross a stream or river, select your crossing point with care, and use a stick to probe the bottom ahead of you as you cross. If you get stuck in some muck or quicksand in water - even if it's not deep enough to drown you, you'll either get hypothermia or starve to death if stuck long enough. Learn how to use and carry a compass so you don't get lost or inadvertently wander into a dangerous area. Avoid moving at night if you can. Rest frequently, so fatigue doesn't make you clumsy. Treat cuts and abrasions as quickly as possible to avoid the chance of infection.

Survival in difficult conditions is a challenge that requires your focus and attention at all times. Under the wrong conditions, the greatest threat to your security could be yourself.

42

ENERGY & HEAT

Unless conditions are extreme, you can survive without heat. Technically, without energy either, but there are bound to be times when you'll need light. Hopefully, you've prepared for this by purchasing several flashlights with onboard generators, as mentioned earlier.

For a permanent shelter (if you have the means), you can invest in a generator, solar panels or a windmill. There's nothing wrong with this, but each has its drawbacks that you need to consider before deciding.

Power from Generators: Generators need fuel. Unless you have the ability to store a significant quantity, you won't be getting power from a generator for very long. Generators also make noise. If you're running a generator, and someone is nearby, they will likely assume you have resources and could pay you a visit. The generator unit itself can be expensive, and unless you're an electrician, the installation will be expensive as well. Given the chance that you might have to evacuate your shelter, and abandon that investment, you'll have to decide if such an investment is worth the trouble.

Power from Solar Panels: Solar panels have numerous advantages over generators, but have some disadvantages of their own as well. They're quiet, and as long as they remain undamaged, they will continue to produce power indefinitely. But again, they're expensive (especially in sufficient quantities to provide adequate power) and unless you have the know-how, they will have to be installed (also not cheap). Of course, solar panels only produce power when the sun is shining, and are vulnerable to damage from storms. They're visible, so the chance exists that they might attract attention from someone who is clever and recognizes them for what they are.

Power from Windmills: These are pretty much in the same realm as solar panels. They only produce power in certain conditions, are susceptible to storm damage, are visible and can be very expensive. None the less, like solar panels, they are a continuous source of power for as long as they last.

43

PETS

Many people are pet lovers, and couldn't imagine abandoning their pets in an emergency. Not to offend anyone's sensibilities, but if you own a cat or a dog, they're not just good companions; they can be valuable survival tools. Dogs can usually detect the approach of a stranger long before we can, barking a warning to alert us to someone whose presence we might not otherwise notice.

As you're probably aware, dogs also have a fantastic sense of smell. If you're having trouble finding food, just walk your dog. Believe me, if there's some food or game around (with the exception of things like plants or mushrooms), your dog will sniff it out and lead you to it even if he isn't trained to do so.

Cats can be particularly useful in your permanent shelter. They will control any mice or vermin that happen to get in, and discourage them from coming around in the first place.

Please forgive this - but any animal can also be a source of food in an extreme crisis.

On the flip side of that, animals do make great companions. If you're constantly alone in a survival situation, this will have a detrimental affect on your morale and well-being. For this reason, and the utilitarian reasons listed above (in spite of the extra drain on your food and water resources), pets are a recommended part of any survival plan - even if you're not a dog or cat person.

44

BUILDING MATERIALS

For your permanent shelter, as previously advised, you might need to make repairs to prevent ongoing damage or collapse. Stock up on:

- Lumber, both plywood and studs
- Piping
- Electrical wire, tape and connectors
- Caulk for sealing leaks
- Nails and screws
- Various hand tools (Non-electric)
- A propane torch and solder (Dual use item; propane can be used for cooking with a camp stove)

Think about the supplies you need to make repairs on your house now. Then remember that in a crisis, those supplies won't be available. Stock up on those things.

If you can, store enough materials to construct an entirely separate shelter near your main shelter, in case your primary one is lost to fire, storm, etc.

Make sure you have a comprehensive set of tools (not power tools of course, manually operated ones). Tools for woodworking or plumbing and mechanic's tools are invaluable. You might have machinery, or could come across useful machinery in need of repair. It's also good to have duplicates of the tools in your kit in case one should break.

45

TRADE GOODS

Earlier we covered security. Lots of books do this, and it's important to remain vigilant. However, few guides mention the fact that humans are social creatures, and we're not all bad. In fact, most of us are pretty decent. In an emergency situation, not every person will be a threat (although, you should always be careful, just in case). Other people could even hold the potential to enhance our security.

Along those lines, it can be a good idea to stock trade goods. It's possible that someone near you has also prepared for a disaster, just with a different philosophy about supplies. Now, they have things you need, and you have things they need. A couple of things that could end up having good trading value besides the usual like food and water, is alcohol and tobacco.

Disasters are a stressful thing. Most people would jump at the chance to have a drink or a cigarette. If you decide to stock trade goods of this nature, it can become a problem for you if you're not careful. You'd better be sure that YOU can handle the temptation when under stress. Smoking is a known threat for the long term. Drinking can be dangerous for reasons ranging from falling down and hurting yourself when drunk, to alcohol poisoning.

If you elect to keep alcohol on hand for trade, get liquors or wine, not beer. The wine and liquor will keep forever and are palatable without being chilled. Beer can spoil, and tastes better cold. Liquor can also be used to clean a wound, should the need arise.

If you're traveling alone, consider the advantages if you met up with another trustworthy individual. If you fall or get hurt, someone is there to assist you. It's much easier to construct a shelter or pitch a tent with two people as opposed to just one. And, of course, there's companionship. Having another human being to talk to, to share in the dangers you face, is very beneficial to your morale and overall mental well-being.

Imagine if you saw a starving fellow unthinkingly taking food from your garden. What if you simply shot him without warning, only to discover that he was a doctor, electrician or farmer. Valuable skills that he might have been happy to share with you, are now lost. If he had friends or family nearby, you have also now made an enemy or enemies.

In normal, everyday life, we suffer the consequences of bad decisions all the time. But modern society protects us from most of the extreme consequences when we make mistakes. In a crisis, when survival is threatened, every little action and every minor decision can quickly become life or death. As a final note, don't underestimate the value of good community. Build one now BEFORE you need it, then if the time comes, that community will serve you in many invaluable ways. A good community is not only useful as a morale booster should times get tough, it can also provide you with greater skills, support and knowledge.

CONCLUSION

I hope you have found this book both useful and enjoyable to read. Aside from the preparation I have repeatedly stressed in this book, I sincerely hope that you never have to use these guidelines. None the less, modern society is marvelously fragile. Natural disasters, pandemics and economic collapse are very real scenarios that we may have to face in our lifetime. Under the right conditions, it wouldn't take much to bring civilization to its knees. All the things that we've depended on for our survival could be wiped out almost instantly.

Being ready in advance - being PREPARED with the right supplies, tools and skills is your best, and possibly only hope for survival. Thanks again, dear reader, for your time. Take care, good luck and God bless.

ABOUT THE AUTHOR

David Pearson has over 10 years experience in emergency and survival training from the oil and gas industry. He left his field after witnessing the startling devastation and impact that drilling is taking on our planet, its communities and natural resources.

His greatest passion is being outdoors and learning new ways to tread lightly. He lives on a homestead in Oregon with his wife, two children and his dog Ernie.

MORE BY DAVID PEARSON

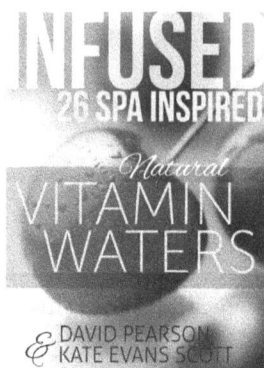

Available Now on Amazon

NOTES

NOTES

NOTES

www.ingramcontent.com/pod-product-compliance
Lightning Source LLC
Chambersburg PA
CBHW071623040426
42452CB00009B/1463